Made in the USA
Las Vegas, NV
15 March 2022

45703617R00057